Jesus' Beach Breakfast

The story of the great catch of fish,
John 21:1–19, for children

Written by Stephenie Hovland
Illustrated by Dave Hill

CONCORDIA PUBLISHING HOUSE • SAINT LOUIS

In Galilee, down by the sea,
Sat James and John (of Zebedee).
Then Thomas and Nathanael, too,
With Simon Peter made a crew.

When Peter planned a fishing trip,
The men got in their little ship.
All night they cast their nets around,
But not one single fish was found.

The sun began to spread its rays;
So soon the dark would go away.
A stranger stood upon the beach.
They knew Him not but heard His speech.

The man asked, "Any fish just yet?"
They had nothing but empty nets.
"Try casting nets off to the right!"
They threw the nets with all their might.

And soon they saw a big surprise!
The nets held fish of every size.
They caught more fish than they could count.
They tugged—amazed at the amount.

Then John was first to realize
It was the Lord before their eyes.
Though they all looked out toward the sand,
Poor Peter could not wait for land.

When Peter knew it was the Lord,
He grabbed his cloak, jumped overboard,
And rapidly he splashed and raced
To see his Savior face-to-face.

So drenched and dripping, Peter went
To be with Christ, whom God had sent.
The others soon came to the beach.
They also hoped to hear Him teach.

A breakfast Jesus had prepared.
Humility and love He shared
With roasted, smoky fish and bread,
And all disciples were well-fed.

Just after breakfast time was done,
Jesus met Peter one-on-one.
"Do you love Me?" Jesus asked.
And Peter thought about his past.

This time Peter needed to show
His love. He said, "Yes, Lord, You know."
Then Jesus answered, "Feed My lambs."
(The Lord would soon tell him His plans.)

That wasn't enough. Christ asked once more.
And Peter answered like before:
"Lord, You know," with love so deep.
The Lord then said, "Go feed My sheep."

Then Jesus asked him one last time,
"Peter, tell Me, is your love Mine?"
Peter sighed, and said, "Lord, I weep.
I do love You!" "Then feed My sheep."

"Come, follow Me," the Savior said.
"Come, follow Me. For you, I've shed
My blood to cleanse you from your sin.
Now all your work will soon begin."

This fisherman would shepherd all
God's people whom the Spirit called.
He'd lead the people faithfully
And write letters for all to read.

Dear Parent,

After a long night of hard work with nothing to show for it, the fishermen see a man on the shore, who tells them to cast their nets on the other side of their small boat. Simple as that. Perhaps in the hope of pulling in something, anything, so their effort wasn't a complete waste, they cast and are richly rewarded. It is John who recognizes the Lord. And impetuous, enthusiastic Peter jumps from the boat to get to Him.

It's notable for us that this is the third time Jesus appeared to His disciples after His resurrection, and He asks Peter three times if he loves Him. Peter had denied Jesus three times, and now declares his love for Jesus three times. Jesus graciously reinstates Peter and gives him—and us—a directive: "Feed My sheep" (John 21:17).

Not only can Peter and the other disciples feed many people with the fish they have just caught, they are now called to preach, baptize, and absolve in Jesus' name. Peter and the other disciples are the first pastors— fishers of men and shepherds—who feed their sheep with the words of Jesus and minister to them.

This Bible story, which is the last lesson Jesus taught His disciples face-to-face, reminds us that just as Jesus fed His disciples on the shore that morning, He continues to feed us through His body and blood in the Holy Supper and through the Bible.

Jesus' directive is for parents and children, too, in that He calls us to share both the bounty we are blessed with and the faith He has given us.

May God bless you and your family as you are fed by His Word and share it with others.

The editor